Earth Alert

Andrew Whitmore

sundance

Published by Sundance Publishing
P.O. Box 1326, 234 Taylor Street, Littleton, MA 01460

Copyright © text Andrew Whitmore

First published 1999 as Phenomena by
Horwitz Martin
A Division of Horwitz Publications Pty Ltd
55 Chandos St., St. Leonards NSW 2065 Australia

Exclusive United States Distribution: Sundance Publishing

ISBN 0-7608-4950-1

Printed in Canada

Contents

Tornado Scale

	Intensity	mph	Damage done
F0	Gale	40–72	Damage to chimneys and store signs; branches broken off trees
F1	Moderate	73–112	Surface peeled off roofs; mobile homes knocked over; cars pushed off roads
F2	Significant	113–157	Roofs torn off lightly built houses; mobile homes demolished; large trees snapped off or uprooted
F3	Severe	158–206	Roofs and walls torn off well-built houses; trains blown over; most trees in forests uprooted
F4	Devastating	207–260	Well-built houses levelled; buildings with weak foundations blown some distance; cars thrown through the air
F5	Incredible	261–318	Strongly built houses disintegrated; cars tossed more than 100 yards; bark stripped from trees; steel reinforced buildings badly damaged
F6	Inconceivable	319–379	No tornado this severe has yet been recorded.

Volcano Alert Rating

Zero	Quiet state
One	First or minor signs of volcanic unrest, no significant eruption threat
Two	Volcano unrest, local eruption threat
Three	Increased volcano unrest, possibility of larger eruption(s)
Four	Large-scale eruption(s) predicted
Five	Large-scale eruption in progress

Author's Note

My own brush with disaster during the 1983 Ash Wednesday fires in Victoria, Australia was a close one. But it made me think. Until then, I suppose I'd always believed that things like that happened to other people. . . .

I've wandered through the ruins of Pompeii. I've climbed Mount Vesuvius. I've traveled on a motorboat across the 3,500-year-old caldera at Santorini. I've also visited Pudding Lane in London, where the Great Fire started. Each time, I couldn't help but wonder what it must have been like to experience such devastating events firsthand.

The only way to do that now, of course, is in our imagination. I hope this book at least partly succeeds in bringing these disasters to life.

Andrew Whitmore has been writing ever since he could hold a pen. Science fiction and fantasy stories are his favorite. Several of his stories have appeared in anthologies and magazines. He has published two novels.

Introduction

I T's EASY to forget that nature can be unpredictable, dangerous, and powerful.

Oceans can suddenly rise up in killer waves that drown whole cities. Mountains can erupt in fire or bury us in tons of rock. The ground can tremble beneath our feet. In the blink of an eye, our homes and loved ones can be wiped from the face of the Earth.

People once used to blame superhuman powers for natural disasters like floods, fires, and earthquakes. Even today, insurance companies call them "Acts of God."

We now understand more about how and why these kinds of events occur. But that doesn't make them any less frightening and unpredictable. Wherever you live, there's a chance that one day you too will experience the awesome destructive power of nature.

What will you do?

How would you deal with nature's fatal fury?

Imagine . . .

Jarrell, Texas
Tuesday, May 27, 1997
3:45 P.M.

B.J.'s MOTHER clutched the phone so tightly her knuckles went white.

"Who is it?" B.J. asked anxiously. "Is something wrong?"

Her mother muttered something, then slammed the receiver down. "That was your dad," she said. She took a deep breath, to calm herself. "He was calling from his truck

on the interstate. He says we've gotta get out of here. There's a tornado headed our way."

B.J. felt a cold knot of fear in her stomach.

8

She'd heard the warnings on the radio. All afternoon, mountains of black clouds had been piling up in the sky north of their house. That wasn't unusual for this time of year. A tornado had swept through the town when she was just a baby.

B.J. tried to remember the lessons drummed into them in school. "Shouldn't we stay inside?" she asked. "Everyone says that's the safest place. We could hide in the closet or something."

Her mother was in no mood to argue. She'd already gathered up her handbag and was heading for the door. "Your dad knows best," she snapped. "Get moving. He's coming straight over to pick us up."

B.J. grabbed a coat and joined her mother on the porch. The wind was gusting even more strongly now. The wind made the whole house shudder. Trees whipped from side to side in the yard. The clouds to the north had turned greenish-yellow and the air was warm and clammy.

B.J. knew that leaving wasn't right. You weren't supposed to try to outrun a tornado. You had to stay under cover and wait for it to blow over. A twister could break you apart if it caught you out in the open.

Suddenly, she heard a squeal of tires. Engine roaring, her dad's truck screeched to a halt at the end of their driveway. The passenger door flew open. Her dad waved to them frantically. "Come on!" he screamed, barely able to make himself heard over the howl of the wind.

B.J. and her mother raced down the driveway. Her dad took off the moment they were inside. He turned west onto Route 305. Then he glanced anxiously in the rear-view mirror and put his foot to the floor.

When B.J. looked out the back window, she saw a huge funnel of boiling black clouds snaking toward their house. It was moving even faster than their truck and roaring like a dozen runaway freight trains. Trees and fences were being sucked right out of the ground.

The twister seemed almost alive, darting from side to side and chewing up everything in its path. B.J. watched it lift whole houses and smash them into a thousand pieces. Cars and farm machines were thrown around like toys. B.J. didn't like to think what it would do to her dad's truck.

"What if it follows us?" she asked.

"It's not gonna follow us," her father said, but he didn't sound so sure. "And if it does, we'll outrun it. Even a twister that size has gotta wear itself out sooner or later."

B.J. hoped he was right. She hunched forward, willing the truck to go faster. Her dad fought the wheel as the wind buffeted them from one side of the road to the other. He had the headlights on high, but she could still barely see where they were going.

B.J. clutched her mother's hand. It was hard to say which of them was trembling more. Please, she thought, don't let us die. Not like this.

They drove on through the darkness, the twister roaring and raging behind them. . . .

Chapter 1
Killer Winds

I MADE UP B.J. and her parents, but everything else in the story you've just read is true.

Tornadoes are the most violent storms on Earth. The swirling winds inside a twister's funnel can reach speeds of over 300 mph (miles per hour). That's strong enough to lift a house right off its foundation. Even concrete buildings are no match for a Force 5 tornado like the one that struck Jarrell, Texas.

Although the Jarrell twister touched down for less than 20 minutes, it left behind a trail of destruction a mile long and one-third of a mile wide. The tiny town of 400 people was nearly wiped out. The twister killed 29 people and injured dozens more.

Fifty homes vanished almost without a trace. In many places, only a bare concrete slab remained to show where a house had been. An 18-wheeler was smashed to pieces 325 yards from where

tornado: A funnel-shaped storm spinning at extremely high speed.

it had been parked. Two-ton pieces of farm machinery lay where living rooms had been. One subdivision on the northwest edge of town was completely destroyed.

"It's not there anymore," one deputy reported. "It's just a flat, vacant field."

Only three survivors were pulled from the rubble. Everyone else caught inside when the tornado struck died. Some were ripped apart. Others were shredded by flying glass and metal. It took days to identify all the victims.

Why Do Disasters Keep Happening?

The United States government spends millions of dollars every year on tornado research. The National Weather Service keeps a lookout for potentially dangerous storms 24 hours a day. Though experts can tell when and where tornadoes are most likely to form, it's impossible to predict exactly where they will strike. Tornado warnings are so common in spring and summer that people don't always take them seriously.

Tornadoes can also occur at night, catching people completely unprepared. A dozen people died when a tornado touched down outside Gainesville, Georgia, in the early hours of

March 20, 1998. Not that there was much the people could have done anyway.

Fortunately, tornadoes on the scale of the one that struck Jarrell are rare. Most are much smaller and last for only one or two minutes. Every year, however, killer twisters hit some part of the United States, claiming dozens of lives and causing millions of dollars worth of damage.

What Causes Tornadoes?

Although tornadoes of one kind or another occur all over the world, their major breeding ground is central North America. This is the area known as "Tornado Alley."

Here, masses of warm, moist air from the south collide with cold air moving down from the north. The hot air is trapped and can't rise in the usual way. As a result, huge storm clouds build up. This creates rising columns of hot air called updrafts. If these updrafts manage to punch through the colder air above them, they begin to turn faster and faster. A tornado is born.

Air inside the funnel of a large tornado can rise at speeds of over 190 mph. This works much like the suction in a vacuum cleaner. Once the spout touches the ground, it begins sucking up masses of dirt and rubble. The outside of the tornado is quickly surrounded by a swirling cloud of dust.

Whirlwind Invasions

In April 1974, an army of almost 150 tornadoes raged for two days over the Midwest from Alabama to the Canadian border. Within eight hours, 315 people were dead and $400 million worth of property was destroyed.

The tornadoes struck 11 different states. Ohio was the worst hit. Thirty people died when a tornado ripped through the town of Xenia. The tornado only lasted five minutes, but it leveled half the town. The trail of destruction was four miles long and a mile wide. The winds inside the funnel were so strong they caused whole buildings to explode.

The story was the same in Alabama, Kentucky, Indiana, and Tennessee. In Sugar Valley, Georgia, one tornado picked up a 9-year-old boy who was playing outside. It carried

The spout of a tornado

him nearly 200 yards before dropping him safely to the ground. His mother, father, and two sisters, who were all inside the house, died.

The giant twister that rampaged through the Midwest on March 18, 1925, ranks as one of the largest and most destructive tornadoes ever. It lasted for almost five hours and traveled 200 miles, carving a mile-wide path of destruction through Illinois, Indiana, and Missouri. The tornado left 659 people dead and over 200 people injured.

Granddaddy of All Tornadoes

To date, the strongest tornado recorded struck the Oklahoma City area on May 3, 1999. Scientists

from the University of Oklahoma and the National Severe Storm Center measured wind speeds of over 300 mph. These are the highest wind speeds recorded anywhere on Earth.

About 3,000 homes were damaged or destroyed. The cost of the damage was more than $1 billion. This makes the May 3 tornado also the most destructive tornado ever.

Damage caused by a tornado

Fortunately, because of advance warning systems, many people were able to seek shelter. Still, 41 people died and almost 700 people were injured.

Even Bigger Storms

Weather conditions similar to those that produce tornadoes also create storms more than 600 miles across. These storms develop over the warm oceans near the equator. They are given different names depending on where they occur. Atlantic Ocean storms are called hurricanes. In areas around the Pacific Ocean, they are known as typhoons. Those storms that occur in the Indian Ocean are called cyclones.

What Causes a Hurricane?

Like tornadoes, hurricanes happen when masses of hot, moist air rises and cooler air rushes in to take its place. Because Earth is constantly spinning, this air moves in a circular motion. Huge thunderclouds develop, swirling around the center of the storm at speeds up to 125 mph. A fully developed hurricane pumps out about two million tons of air every second, and it releases more energy than 400 hydrogen bombs.

What Goes On Inside a Hurricane?

Satellite view of a hurricane

At the heart of every hurricane is a tower of hot air several miles wide. This is known as the eye of the storm. In the eye, the wind is light and there is usually no rain at all. The sky may be completely blue.

People caught in a hurricane are often tricked into thinking that the storm has ended when the eye passes over them. But then even fiercer winds sweep in behind it.

Surrounding the eye are huge walls of clouds spiraling inward at enormous speeds. These can unleash as much rain in one day as a city like London receives in a year.

In satellite photographs, hurricanes look like gigantic wheels spinning across the ocean. When they hit the coastline, the results can be devastating.

eye: The calm, cloudless center of a hurricane.

Darwin's Darkest Hour

The people of Darwin, Australia, were settling down to celebrate Christmas Eve in 1974 when they first heard that Cyclone Tracy was headed their way. No one paid much attention. Two weeks before, a cyclone had crossed the coast without causing any damage at all.

A hurricane

The wind gradually strengthened. By midnight, trees were being stripped of leaves and branches snapped. Violent rain poured down on the city. Families huddled together in their bathrooms for safety.

At about 2:30 A.M., the winds died. Although Tracy had already badly damaged many homes, most were still standing. People thought the worst was over. In fact, it was just the eye of the cyclone passing through. The worst was yet to come.

About half an hour later, as the eye passed, much stronger winds began to blow. At the airport, planes were blown from their hangars. Wind meters registered speeds of 133 mph.

Homes were torn from their foundation. Roofs were sent spinning through the air. Fifty people died. They were crushed when their houses collapsed around them or were killed when they were hit by flying debris. Another fifteen died on boats in the Darwin harbor.

Cyclone Tracy ravaged Darwin for six hours. It left behind a city flattened as if it were hit by a nuclear explosion. Seventy percent of the houses were seriously damaged. Over 30,000 people were left homeless.

Disaster of the Century?

Bangladesh is the most densely populated country on Earth. About 800 people are packed into every square mile. Most live on the low mud flats where the Ganges River flows into the Bay of Bengal.

The effects of a cyclone

(The Bay of Bengal is a breeding ground for cyclones.) On November 12, 1970, these factors came together to produce what may be the century's worst natural disaster.

Weather satellites picked up the approaching storm. Warnings were broadcast, but no one took them seriously. Like the people of Darwin, these people had seen a cyclone pass through just a few weeks before. That one hadn't been as bad as they had expected. So this time most people just went to bed.

The storm struck in the middle of the night. Winds of over 200 mph sent a 33-foot-high wall of water crashing across the coastline. The flimsy houses were smashed into piles of wet straw. Lowland areas were completely swamped.

The scene the next morning was one of complete disaster. Dead bodies clogged every stream, dangled from every tree, and lined every beach. On one island alone, more than 20,000 people had disappeared without a trace. In some areas, rescue workers couldn't move without stepping on a dead body. The official government death toll was set at 300,000. But outside observers believe that the actual figure was closer to a million.

Who Will Be Next?

Each year, 250 monster-size tropical storms batter coastlines and claim lives all around the world.

The United States and Japan have developed advanced weather detection systems. Still,

Scientists use satellites to keep track of global weather patterns.

hurricanes and cyclones take people by surprise. Their paths are difficult to predict, even using the most powerful computers. And the tropical storms can change direction without warning. No matter how people prepare, these monster storms will continue to bring death and destruction when they strike.

In October 1998, more than 10,000 people died when Hurricane Mitch swept through Central America. Honduras and Nicaragua were left in ruins. By the time it finally broke off the coast of Florida, Mitch had caused tremendous death and destruction. Hurricane Mitch now ranks as one of the 20th century's deadliest hurricanes.

No matter how advanced our technology becomes, there will always be another Jarrell, Texas, or Hurricane Mitch. Like fires, floods, and other disasters, monster storms remind us just how helpless we are when nature rages.

Chapter 2: Introduction

Imagine . . .

Hawkesdale, southwest Victoria, Australia
Wednesday, February 16, 1983
3:25 P.M.

STRONG WINDS HAD BEEN blowing all day. I was as glad as my students when the bell finally rang. The temperature was well over 100 degrees. We were all drenched with sweat. Wind rattled the classroom windows. I could barely hear myself think. Outside, an eerie light had spread across the sky. It was as if the air itself was glowing.

The students were restless and on edge. They knew what all of this meant. They had seen it many times before and would no doubt see it many times again. But that didn't make it any less frightening.

It was wildfire weather.

No one hung around after school. The parking lot was crowded. Parents had come to pick up their children rather than have them take the bus home as usual.

"Hurry up," I heard one mother shout as she rushed her son into the car. Her face was tense. "There's smoke everywhere."

I hurried home myself. I soon realized the woman had been right. You could smell the smoke, but there was no way to tell where it was coming from. I knew there were fires somewhere—maybe lots of them. I just hoped none were anywhere near us.

By the time I got home, the wind was even stronger. It almost knocked me off my feet as I staggered from the garage to the house.

The air was so hot I felt as if a giant hair dryer were blowing in my face. The sky had darkened by now. If it hadn't been for the smell of smoke, you might have thought it was going to rain. The sun peered down through the haze like an evil red eye.

I was glad to get inside. I'd been worried about my wife and daughter. We live in a farmhouse about ten miles from town. Two years before, there had been a bad fire just a few miles away. Several firefighters had been killed when their truck was engulfed by flames along a nearby dirt road.

We sat and waited for hour after hour. The worst thing was not knowing what was happening. News reports on the radio didn't tell us much. Looking outside didn't help, either. The smoke that constantly swirled around us could have been coming from 30 miles away, or just down the road.

I thought of all the things I should have done. It had been a long, dry summer. Something like this was bound to happen. I should have cleaned the gutters and cleared the brush from around the house. I should have invested in a fire pump.

Born and raised in the city, I'd never given a thought to wildfires—they only happened to other people. Now I was in the middle of one and without the slightest idea what I ought to do about it.

Later that afternoon, the wind changed. For a while, it gusted even more strongly. We could hear it roaring across the roof and shaking the porch. For a while, we thought the whole house was going to blow away.

Then it began to rain.

I have never felt so relieved. As I listened to the water drumming on our roof, I knew we were going to be all right. Even though I'd been too thoughtless to take the proper safety measures, this time I'd gotten away with it.

When I watched the evening news I realized how lucky we'd been. Half of southwest Victoria had gone up in flames. Some of the worst fires had been no more than 20 miles away. Seventy-five people had died. Whole towns had been wiped out. Over 2,000 homes had been burned to the ground.

Ours easily could have been one of them. . . .

Chapter 2
Inferno

Lightning causes many forest fires.

In 1983, Ash Wednesday, a Christian holy day, fell on February 16. It certainly lived up to its name. The fires that blazed across southeastern Australia are known as the Ash Wednesday fires. The story you just read—my own brush with disaster—may not have been too dramatic. But many others weren't so lucky.

The Ash Wednesday fires were the most widespread fires in Australian history. They killed more people and destroyed more homes than any fires before or since. In all, over 864,500 acres of land were burned. That's an area about the same size as 700,000 soccer fields.

Which Forests Burn? And Why?

On October 27, 1993, southern California experienced its own version of the Ash Wednesday fires. But the California fires lasted more than 10 days. Burning on 14 separate fronts, these fires destroyed more than 1,000 buildings and reduced more than 300 square miles of real estate to ashes.

Along with the south of France, California and southeastern Australia are among the most fire-prone regions on Earth. All three areas share much the same climate. In summer, temperatures often rise well above 100°F for days at a time, drying out the vegetation. When the weather is right, one spark is enough to set the blaze.

Many trees in these parts of the world need the intense heat of a forest fire in order for their seeds to sprout. Some of these trees actually produce chemicals that feed the flames. Huge balls of burning gas that extend hundreds of yards ahead of the fire itself can be created.

How Often Do Forests Burn?

vegetation:
Plant life.

Fortunately, disasters on the scale of the Ash Wednesday fires and the California wildfires don't happen often. After a firestorm, it might take forests 40 or 50 years to regrow and pile up enough dead vegetation to fuel another wildfire.

Plenty of other fires occur in between, of course. About 100,000 forest fires are reported every year in the United States. That's 364 a day. The total area burned averages almost 12,000 square miles. Major fires have occurred as far south as Florida and as far north as Alaska.

It's a similar story in Australia. In an average year, 15,000 forest fires burn about 9,000 square miles of land.

A Recipe for Disaster

For a major forest fire to break out, a number of things have to happen. First, the summer has to be unusually dry. This provides the dry fuel the fires need in order to burn so rapidly.

Second, there has to be a strong wind blowing. Any hot, gusty wind is dangerous, but the worst fires occur when the wind is shifting direction.

Third, it needs to be hot.

Fuel, wind, and heat. Add these together, and a wildfire is almost certain to erupt.

How Hot?

The amount of energy unleashed by a major fire is awesome. In forest areas, flames can stretch 200 yards above the treetops and reach temperatures of almost 3,300°F. That's hot enough to melt iron.

The heat produced by a firestorm is so intense it can twist heavy metal and melt fencing wire. During the Ash Wednesday fires, a car in a service station became welded to the hoist it was sitting on.

Just before and after a cold front, huge columns of rising hot air, known as convection columns occur. Convection columns can cause flames to gush up over 650 feet high. When there is a dramatic change in air temperature from where the convection column started to its highest point, a firestorm may form.

Firestorms

Basically, a firestorm is a column of fire that makes an inward wind. The inward wind supplies the oxygen that keeps the firestorm going.

Firestorms are the most dangerous fires on Earth. Their convection columns are sometimes 10,000 or more yards tall and hundreds of yards wide. Inside the firestorm, vertical winds gust to 200 mph. These winds can rip whole trees out of the ground and hurl them through the air. The sounds of exploding gases can be heard miles away.

In full force, firestorms become hungry monsters destroying everything they touch. Gigantic tongues of flame leap out, then draw back. It's as if they are choosing the tastiest parts of the forest to devour. They roar like a jet engine. They spit out burning leaves and burning branches that can start new fires up to 20 miles away.

Every yard of fire-front gives out as much heat as 100,000 electric radiators. Anyone caught unprotected in the path of a fire-front would be killed almost immediately.

What Are the Chances of Survival?

People will always die in forest fires. Those most at risk are the firefighters themselves. They are closest to the fire and can be surrounded by flames or crushed by falling trees. But the odds of surviving even the biggest fire are good if people take the

A forest fire

31

right safety measures.

Although major wildfires give off incredible heat, they also move quickly. If people clear dead vegetation from around their houses, there's little chance the house will catch fire. In fact, most houses burn down *after* the fire-front has passed.

Forest fires can destroy a forest in hours.

Houses catch fire when burning embers collect in roofs and walls. The embers smolder for hours before they finally burst into flames. With a bucket of water and a mop, these small fires can be put out before they spread.

Even if you are caught outside in a forest fire, you can protect yourself. Heat is the main killer. If you can shield your body for the time it takes the fire-front to pass, you will survive. A simple wool blanket soaked in water can mean the difference between life and death.

Burning Cities

It isn't just forests that burn. Some of the worst wildfires have been in cities. This doesn't happen often now because of the building materials used and the development of strong firefighting services.

In the past, horrible fires have made whole cities into piles of smoking ruins and killed thousands of people. Many of these fires were a result of other natural disasters.

A Dark Day for San Francisco

On the morning of April 18, 1906, San Francisco was struck by a severe earthquake. But this was only the beginning of the city's troubles.

Within ten minutes, fires had started all over the city. At first, they started as stoves and gas lamps were broken in the earthquake. One fire broke out when a housewife preparing breakfast outside her collapsed home struck a match. The match lit gas leaking from broken pipes. The resulting fire leveled several blocks of houses.

> earthquake: A tremor of the Earth's crust, usually caused by plates deep underground moving against each other.

Soon 52 separate fires were burning across the city. To make matters worse, the water supply had been cut off by the earthquake. By noon, the whole city was ablaze. The fire raged out of control for almost four days.

Three-quarters of the city was completely destroyed, including over 25,000 buildings. More than 300,000 people were left with nowhere to live.

The Worst Inferno of Them All?

Fire followed the great Tokyo earthquake of 1923. In those days, city buildings were made almost entirely of wood. The earthquake smashed the buildings like matchsticks. Hundreds of fires broke out, most started by coals from overturned stoves. As had happened in San Francisco, water mains were destroyed. So, there was no water to stop the fires from spreading.

Violent winds created the same type of firestorms that occur during major wildfires. More than 24,000 people fled to the safety of a park. They died in a fiery whirlwind that hurled their bodies high into the air. The same thing happened to 40,000 others huddled in the grounds of a warehouse.

Thousands of people who dived for safety into Tokyo harbor also died. Oil tanks in the harbor exploded and spread burning oil over the water. The people there burned to death.

In all, 140,000 people died in the great disaster. Another 100,000 were badly injured. The cities of Tokyo and nearby Yokohama were virtually wiped out.

The Burning of London

Perhaps the most famous fire of all is the one that ravaged London in 1666. Legend says it was started by a careless baker who forgot to put out the fires in his ovens at the end of the day. Minutes after the fire broke out early Sunday, September 26, the whole street was ablaze.

London was a city of rotten wood houses, crammed together on narrow streets. Many of these houses had straw roofs. Once the fire took hold, there was no stopping it. By Monday night, the firey red sky of London could be seen over 40 miles away.

The fire raged for more than four days. Eventually, the wind dropped. People were able to stop the fire from spreading by destroying buildings to form firebreaks.

firebreak: Something, usually an open space, that stops the spread of a fire.

By this time, though, 80 percent of the city was ruined. Amazingly, only a handful of people were killed.

Indonesia's Fires

Indonesia's turn came in 1997. Huge fires blazed out of control on the islands of Borneo and Sumatra for more than four months. The fires burned over 9,300 square miles of forest. Smoke from the fires covered an area larger than all of Europe.

Tomorrow's Firestorm

The world's forests will burn again. If not this summer, then the next. If not in the United States, then somewhere else in the world. I might even live to see fires like the Ash Wednesday fires again.

The forests will regrow, building up new stores of fuel. People will forget the lessons they learned and become careless again. The countryside will dry out. The temperature will soar. The wind will blow.

And then, all it will take is a single spark.

Imagine . . .

St. Pierre, Martinique
Thursday, May 8, 1902
7:30 A.M.

*D*ear Patrick,

It looks as if things are finally beginning to settle down. The sky is clear this morning. Old Mount Pelèe keeps on steaming and grumbling. But I think the worst may be over. We might even go for a picnic.

Mother still wants to leave. I heard her and Father arguing about it last night. He told her that people would laugh at us if we ran away. Besides, he says, there are plenty of ships in the harbor if we need to get out in a hurry.

The mountain has been smoking for weeks now. For a while, you could barely see the sun at all. The air stinks of rotten eggs. Some days the smell was so bad that birds fell out of the sky. We kept the shutters closed to keep from choking ourselves.

There's ash everywhere. It gets in your clothes and your hair and your eyes—even in your food. The gardens look as if they're buried in powdery gray snow.

Mother thinks the whole island is cursed. There's certainly been some strange things happening lately. A plague of snakes slithered into town the other day. The streets were full of them. I heard 50 people were killed.

Further up the mountain, there have been huge swarms of ants and centipedes. It's like something out of the Bible.

All the animals have gone crazy lately. You can hardly sleep at night for all the bleating, and neighing, and bellowing. Maybe they know something we don't.

The government says there's nothing to worry about. I guess they know what they're talking about. Some scientists were sent up the mountain to see what was happening. They don't think there's any real danger at all. They say the mountain's just letting off a little steam, that's all.

But every time I look out my window I see the huge column of smoke towering above us. I can't help but wish that I were somewhere else.

But Father is right, I guess. St. Pierre is our home now. Besides, he has a business to run.

One of the company's sugar mills was buried in a landslide last Monday. He's been working hard ever since to reorganize things. We can't just pack up and leave for no good reason. After all, the governor and his wife are happy enough to stay. There can't be too much to worry about.

And I really do like it here. The weather is beautiful. We have a nice house to live in. I can go swimming whenever I want. A little smoke now and then isn't going to kill me.

Still, I think I'll pray extra hard at church this week, just to be on the safe side.

Mother's calling me now. I have to go. Hope you and your family are keeping well. Say hello to everyone at school for me.

Yours sincerely,

Edward

P.S. Write soon. I'm dying to hear more about the new principal. He sounds even meaner and smellier than Mount Pelèe! . . .

Chapter 3
Fire Mountain

Even if a letter like the one you just read was written, we wouldn't be able to read it. Shortly before 8:00 A.M. on the morning of May 8, 1902, Mount Pelèe erupted with terrifying force.

The explosion was heard 900 miles away and ripped the entire mountain apart. Within minutes, a huge cloud of burning gas and white-hot ash engulfed the town. Almost all of the 30,000 people living there died instantly. Ships in the harbor overturned and their crews were boiled alive.

The heat of the fireball was so intense it melted glass, twisted steel, and turned wood to charcoal. The explosion tore apart yard-thick stone and cement walls like they were cardboard.

Only four survivors were found. Three of them died soon after. If Edward had existed, both he and his letter would have been burned to ashes.

The eruption of Mount Pelèe is regarded as the most devastating volcanic eruption ever.

The Furnace Below Our Feet

The ground we stand on isn't as solid as it looks. Earth's surface is actually in pieces, called plates, that fit together like huge paving stones. The plates float on a sea of white-hot rock known as the mantle. Just 125 miles below our feet, the temperature is hot enough to melt iron.

Volcanoes like Mount Pelèe are formed from pockets of molten rock. The molten rock, called magma, pushes its way up through weak spots in Earth's crust and erupts as lava.

Where Are the Danger Zones?

Volcanic eruptions usually happen where two plates meet. If the plates are moving apart, as they do near Iceland in the Arctic Circle, a crack opens up and magma rises to fill the gap. These eruptions of magma to fill a gap take place constantly and form a series of ridges.

Other eruptions occur where two plates collide. The edge of one plate

plates: Sections of Earth's crust that are constantly moving and changing.

magma: The super-heated rock inside the earth.

gets pushed down closer to the mantle and begins to heat up. As the rocky crust melts, it becomes magma, which then forces its way back to the surface. This happens most often along the "Ring of Fire." That is where the plate carrying the entire Pacific Ocean is slowly grinding its way into six other plates.

A third kind of eruption takes place over hot spots in the mantle. These hot spots produce enough magma to punch a hole right through a plate. The Hawaiian Islands in the Pacific Ocean were made from volcanoes formed in this way.

The only continent that has no active volcanoes is Australia. This is because it sits right in the middle of a plate far away from any hot spots.

Why So Many Shapes and Sizes?

Not all volcanoes look like mountains. Where plates are moving apart, lava often pours out from long cracks in Earth's surface.

In other places, a rising column of magma creates a cone shape. The lava gushes up and spreads out in a circle around the central hole, or vent, and begins to harden. The

crust: The thin outer layer of rock around Earth.

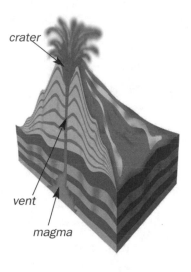

crater

vent

magma

A cone-shaped volcano

hardening lava gets buried beneath millions of tons of ash and cinders.

Each time the volcano erupts, new layers are added. More lava flows down the side of the cone, like icing over a cake, and more ash falls.

The top of the cone almost always collapses back into the vent to form a dish-shaped crater. When a crater fills with water, it becomes a crater lake.

When lava flows continue for a long time without explosions of ash, a much broader and lower dome builds up. These are called shield volcanoes.

caldera: A large, crater formed when the sides of a volcano collapse, or when the top blows off during an eruption.

Sometimes, almost the entire center of the cone collapses or is blown up in a huge eruption. What's left behind is a caldera many miles across.

A Mountain Blows Its Top

The most violent eruptions happen when a volcano's vent becomes plugged. When this happens, the magma below begins to build up pressure. When this pressure is

Volcano crater

finally released, the entire volcano can blow apart, the way Mount Pelèe did. Much the same thing happened to Mount St. Helens in Washington State.

For several years, scientists had been predicting that Mount St. Helens would erupt violently one day. But they had no idea exactly when. An observation post was set up on the north face of the mountain so that the build-up to the eruption could be studied at close range.

This Is It!

At 8:32 in the morning of May 18, 1980, an urgent message came from David Johnson. Johnson was manning the observation post on Mount St. Helens.

Before, during, and after the eruption of Mt. St. Helens

"This is it," he said. "The mountain's going." A moment later he was dead. The entire north side of Mount St. Helens had exploded with the force of 10 million tons of TNT. The size and suddenness of the eruption surprised everyone.

The explosion lasted for nine hours. Hundreds of square miles of forest were flattened. Melted ice created a mud flow, or lahar, 30 miles wide that raced down the mountain at speeds up to 95 mph.

Millions of tons of ash roared from the crater, rising to a height of 13 miles. Towns 185 miles away were blanketed with ash. Snowplows had to be used to clear the roads for emergency vehicles.

Thanks to the safety measures that had been taken, only 61 people were killed in the blast. But about two million animals were destroyed. Enough trees were knocked down to build 250,000 homes.

Bad Luck or a Bad Mistake?

Scientists hope eventually to learn enough about the mysteries of nature to predict eruptions accurately. Unfortunately, scientists couldn't help the villagers of Armero in northern Colombia, when a nearby volcano, Nevado del Ruiz, erupted in 1985.

Experts thought that there was a 67 percent chance the volcano might erupt. If it did, the melting ice and snow would cause a gigantic mudslide, like the one at Mount St. Helens. Scientists believed, however, that the mud would move very slowly. They thought there would be time to get people out of the valleys below.

Nevado del Ruiz began rumbling and spitting fire around 4 P.M. on November 13. Radio broadcasts urged everyone to remain calm. Six hours later, the mountain blew.

Super-heated magma exploded through the vent. The snowcap on the mountain boiled instantly, sending millions of gallons of scalding hot mud and water down the mountainside. The 160-foot-high wave of mud and water flattened trees and set fire to everything in its path. Before anyone knew what was happening, Armero and most of its 25,000 people had disappeared under a sea of molten mud.

The next day, only 4,000 villagers were found

alive. Many of them had been trapped in their houses as the mud cooled and hardened around them.

With a final death toll of around 25,000—including 8,000 children—the Nevado del Ruiz eruption ranks alongside Mount Pelèe as one of the worst volcanic disasters of the 20th century.

The Biggest and Loudest?

The two largest eruptions ever recorded both happened on islands that are now part of Indonesia. This area is unstable because five plates are all grinding into each other at the same time.

Tamboro

The first eruption took place in April 1815. The giant volcano known as Tamboro, near Java, blew its top. The eruption killed nearly 49,000 people. It threw 1.7 million tons of ash and rock into the air—enough to build three mountains as big as the tallest mountains in Europe.

Most of the ash and rock fell to Earth within a few hours. The rest was ground into fine dust like baby powder and rose high into the atmosphere. This dust cloud circled Earth for months.

Krakatoa: the Loudest?

The volcanic island of Krakatoa, west of Java, exploded in 1883. At 10:02 A.M. on August 27, three-quarters of the island collapsed into the magma chamber below. Sea-water rushed in over the island and immediately turned to steam. The explosion this caused was heard 3,000 miles away. It was the loudest sound ever heard by humans.

Huge chunks of volcanic rock were scattered over 900 miles of ocean. Shock waves circled the world three times. Over 36,000 people died. Many of them were drowned when the 115-foot waves caused by the explosion smashed across the coasts of nearby islands.

Lost Cities

Perhaps the most famous volcanic eruption of all was that of Mount Vesuvius in southern Italy. It is not famous because of how much it destroyed, but because of what it preserved.

Mount Vesuvius erupted on August 24, in the year 79 A.D. The nearby Roman cities of Pompeii and Herculaneum were buried beneath many feet of ash and lava. For almost 1,800 years the two cities were forgotten. At the beginning of the 18th century, however, archaeologists digging the area made amazing discoveries.

Both cities seemed almost frozen in time. In Pompeii, ash and volcanic dust had covered the victims like wet cement. Though the bodies inside had decayed, their exact shape was saved by the rock that had hardened around them. An Italian archaeologist made plaster figures from these molds.

These plaster figures show us exactly how the people of Pompeii died. Most appear to have been suffocated by the clouds of poisonous gas that came from Vesuvius that afternoon. They can be seen holding hands and cloths to their mouths, or gasping for breath.

Many were found near the sea, struck down as they tried to escape. Others didn't even try. One soldier was still standing to attention at his post. Another man had died fighting off five others who appeared to be trying to rob him. He was found with a sword in one hand and his foot resting on a pile of silver and gold.

Nature's Time Bombs

Volcanoes will always erupt. Scientists can now tell when a major eruption is brewing. What they cannot tell is how violent it will be or how much damage it will cause. Even when a volcano is known to be active, many people turn a blind eye to the danger.

The city of Naples is only a few miles from Mount Vesuvius. Vesuvius has erupted 40 times over the years since Pompeii and Herculaneum were destroyed. But the threat of another eruption hasn't stopped 1.5 million Italians from living in Naples.

In the story at the beginning of this chapter, Edward's father should have listened to his wife. Instead, he ignored the danger signs. The only way to survive when a volcano like Mount Pelèe blows its top is not to be around when it happens.

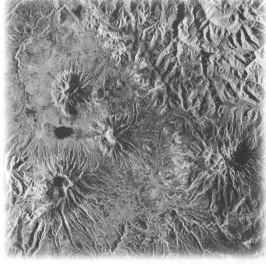

A satellite image of volcanoes in Ecuador

Chapter 4: Introduction

Imagine . . .

Kobe, Japan
Tuesday, January 17, 1995
5:46 A.M.

Satomi couldn't move her legs. She couldn't see them either. The air was choked with dust. Now that the roaring had stopped, the house seemed deathly silent. All Satomi could hear were a few creaks and her own breathing.

For a split second, she hadn't realized what was happening. One moment she was fast asleep. The next moment she was bouncing

around as if on a giant trampoline. Things kept falling on top of her. The noise was deafening. It seemed to go on forever, although it couldn't have lasted for more than a minute.

Nothing she'd learned at school had prepared her for this. They had earthquake drills every month. Don't panic, Mr. Tamose had said. Get under something solid like a table or a doorway. By the time Satomi knew what was happening, she couldn't even see the door, let alone reach it.

She forced herself to think—How do I get out of here?

She had to free her legs. She fumbled for her flashlight. As she shone it around the room, she saw all four walls had buckled like a crumpled cardboard box. Clothes and toys were everywhere. A bookcase had wedged itself across the bottom of her bed and over her legs. Straining every muscle, she finally managed to wriggle her legs out from under it. She'd been lucky. Another few inches and the bookcase would have crushed her legs completely.

Wincing with pain, she hobbled out into the corridor. Her brother's room was right next door. She decided to check there first. Hisao was huddled in a corner, clutching his favorite teddy bear. He wasn't even crying, just staring silently into space.

"You okay?" she asked.

Hisao looked at her for a moment, then nodded. Satomi took his hand and helped him up. "Don't worry," she said gently. "You're safe now. Let's go find Mama and Papa."

Hisao glanced down at his teddy bear. "Miko, too?"

"Sure," Satomi said. "Now hold tight. We don't want you getting lost."

Part of the ceiling had caved in just a few yards from Hisao's room. They had to climb over broken tiles and heaps of fallen plaster to reach the stairs. Halfway down, another tremor struck.

Although it was nowhere near as strong as the first one, Satomi still needed to grab hold of the railing to stop herself from falling. Hisao threw his arms around her leg and hung on for dear life.

As soon as the shaking stopped, Satomi scooped him up and raced for the front door. She'd learned enough about earthquakes to know there could be another aftershock any moment. The next one might bring the whole house down.

"Where's Mama and Papa?" Hisao asked.

Satomi glanced down the hall to her parents' room. There was no sound from the room. It was blocked with rubble. Wires dangled from the exposed rafters. She could smell gas in the air. There was no time. They had to get out now.

"They're waiting outside," Satomi lied. "Now, just be quiet."

She didn't stop running until she reached the railroad line at the end of the street. The tracks were twisted like strands of spaghetti. She put Hisao down, then gazed back at the rows of shattered buildings. It looked as if a giant had stomped on them. One block of apartments had collapsed. Clouds of smoke drifted above the ruins.

She waited for other people to appear, but no one did.

Hisao stared too. "All fall down," he said.

Satomi started to cry. She put her arms around Hisao and held him tight. "Yes," she said quietly. "All fall down." . . .

Chapter 4
The Quaking Earth

Satomi's story is fiction. But the earthquake that struck Kobe on January 17, 1995, left the people of Japan feeling stunned and helpless. About 5,500 people died in the disaster and 170,000 buildings were destroyed. Total damage was about $100 billion. There had been nothing like it in Japan since the great earthquake of 1923.

The Kobe region was supposed to be one of the most stable areas in the country. Until 1995, most serious earthquakes had been centered off the coast, like the one that destroyed Tokyo in 1923.

The Kobe earthquake

Besides, Japan has strict regulations to make sure that buildings are strong enough to survive earthquake damage. Suddenly, the 6th largest city in Japan looked like a war zone. It seemed beyond belief.

Cracked Plates

Like volcanoes, most earthquakes occur along the edges of the vast plates that make up Earth's surface. The islands of Japan sit right on top of four colliding plates. That is why earthquakes are common there.

Earthquakes, however, also occur along cracks within the plates themselves, known as faults. Earthquakes along a fault aren't usually as strong as when plates collide, because only the top layers of rock move. Still the shock waves are so close to the surface that they can cause even worse damage to buildings. Unfortunately for Kobe, a 35-mile fault ran directly under the city.

A fault may only become active every few thousand years. People may not even know a fault is there.

The earthquake that claimed 12 lives and seriously damaged 35,000 homes in Newcastle, Australia, on December 28, 1989, was a complete surprise. Australian cities were thought to be safe from earthquakes. The country

fault: A weak point inside Earth's crust.

shock wave: A burst of energy released from rocks inside the Earth.

is located away from the world's major earthquake zones.

A Disaster Waiting to Happen?

The most famous fault line in the world, the San Andreas fault, runs through California. Here the North American and Pacific Plates are sliding in opposite directions at the rate of 2.3 inches a year. Pressure build-ups along the San Andreas fault have caused several major earthquakes in the region.

San Francisco has experienced the power of a killer quake already. In 1906, an earthquake centered almost directly underneath the Golden Gate Bridge destroyed large parts of the city and sparked fires that burned the rest of it to the ground. Experts calculate that another earthquake the same size would leave 50,000 people dead.

The quake that struck on October 17, 1989, wasn't anywhere near that bad. Even so, the disaster claimed 67 lives and left widespread destruction.

LA Shakers

At 4:31 A.M. on Monday, January 17, 1994, Los Angeles received a nasty jolt of its own. Although the earthquake wasn't particularly powerful, it was still the most damaging to hit the United States since 1906.

Fifty-seven people were killed and more than 1,500 people were seriously injured. About 12,500 buildings were either completely or partly destroyed.

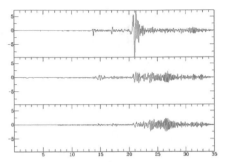

A seismograph measures movements in Earth's crust.

If the quake had struck during working hours, the death toll would have been much higher. A similar quake struck Los Angeles in 1971, but it did less damage because it happened in a less populated area.

How Long?

Scientists use sensitive instruments called seismographs to record the shock waves produced by earthquakes. Although shock waves can be extremely powerful, they don't last very long.

The earthquake that rocked Kobe was over in 20 seconds. The longest U.S. quake on record was the great earthquake that hit Alaska on March 27, 1964. Even then, the shaking only lasted for four minutes.

How Strong?

Information from seismographs allows scientists to calculate how much energy an earthquake releases. This is known as the magnitude of the earthquake. Magnitude is rated according to a scale invented by the American scientist Charles F. Richter in 1935. The Newcastle earthquake of 1989, for example, measured 5.6 on the Richter scale.

People sometimes think the Richter scale gives a score out of ten. The Richter scale actually measures the size of the shock waves produced by an earthquake. Each whole number represents a shock wave ten times larger than the one before it. The 6.7 shock waves from the quake that struck Los Angeles in 1994 were more than ten times stronger than the 5.7 shock waves felt in Newcastle, Australia. They also released over 31 times as much energy.

How Bad?

magnitude:
Size or degree;
scope.

The Richter scale only measures how powerful an earthquake is. It does not measure how much shaking it causes. How badly the ground shakes is called the intensity of the earthquake.

The power of an earthquake depends on exactly where it hits. The intensity depends on how close an earthquake is to the surface and the kind of rock it passes through. Since the intensity is what causes the damage, it is important to measure it as well.

Intensity can't be measured by machines. Investigators have to look at the after-effects of an earthquake and see how much damage it caused. The most common way of recording earthquake intensity is the Modified Mercalli Intensity Scale.

Mercalli Scale

The Mercalli scale describes the effects of different kinds of earthquakes and gives each of them a number. On the Mercalli scale, the numbers range from one to twelve. Roman numerals are used so these numbers won't be confused with the Richter numbers.

Earthquakes measuring I on the scale aren't felt by most people, but are still detected by seismographs. On the other hand, an intensity XII earthquake would completely destroy every building, and cause the earth to buckle.

Whole Lot of Shakin' Going On

Earth's plates are constantly quivering, like a bowl of jelly. Most of the time we aren't aware of those movements. Only a fraction of them are strong enough for us to notice.

Scientists record about 10,000 minor quakes every day. Each year, there are at least 800 quakes as strong as or stronger than the Newcastle earthquake, and 18 the size of the Kobe quake. Monster earthquakes, with a magnitude of 8 or higher, happen about once a year.

Earthquake Belts

About 80 percent of monster earthquakes (higher than 8) happen in an earthquake belt that circles the Pacific, called the "Ring of Fire." A second major earthquake belt runs from Indonesia through the Himalayan mountains and across the Mediterranean Sea.

Some of the worst earthquakes of recent years have hit this second belt. Two of the most devastating include the Iranian earthquake that claimed over 12,000 lives in August 1968, and the Armenian earthquake that killed over 25,000 people on December 7, 1988.

The same belt passes through central China, one of the most densely populated regions on Earth. Earthquakes have killed more people in China than in the rest of the world put together.

Land of the Killer Quakes

On January 23, 1556, China suffered the worst earthquake disaster ever recorded. The quake, which struck the northern province of Shensi, left more than 830,000 people dead. Most of them lived in caves dug from a hillside. They were asleep when the earthquake struck. The entire hill collapsed on top of them.

The nightmare repeated 420 years later.

It happened just before 4 A.M. on July 28, 1976. The Chinese city of Tangshan was jolted by a massive earthquake measuring 8.2 on the Richter scale. Another earthquake almost as big struck 16 hours later. The shock waves were so powerful that they cracked plaster and shattered windows 90 miles away in the Chinese capital of Beijing.

When details of the disaster were finally released, they stunned the world. Over 655,000 people had died. Another 780,000 were seriously injured. Tangshan itself was completely destroyed. A full year after the quake, a foreign visitor said it still looked like the site of an atomic bomb blast.

Taken together, the Shensi and Tangshan disasters killed more people in just two days than all of the earthquakes in the last 200 years.

The Deadliest Disaster of All?

A major earthquake can do more than just knock down houses. Loose soil can be shaken so badly it begins to act almost like water. This is called liquefaction. People in San Francisco during the 1906 earthquake reported seeing whole buildings sucked into the ground, as if the ground were quicksand.

In mountain areas, earthquakes can also cause avalanches and landslides. Whole towns and villages have been destroyed in this way. In cities, the fires that earthquakes help start often cause far more deaths than the earthquakes themselves. That's what happened in both San Francisco in 1906 and Tokyo in 1923. When they occur under or close to the sea, earthquakes may trigger giant ocean waves that devastate low-lying areas thousands of miles away.

liquefaction: During the intense shaking of an earthquake, solid material such as soil begins to act like a liquid.

It is estimated that, in one way or another, earthquakes have caused more than 13 million deaths over the last 4,000 years. No other natural disaster strikes so suddenly—or so often. Nothing else can quite compare with the sheer destructive power of an earthquake.

This lake was formed by an earthquake.

Our Unstable Future

Every day, millions of people run the risk of experiencing the power of a killer earthquake. Tokyo, Los Angeles, and San Francisco are among the world's largest cities. All of them have been rocked by earthquakes in the past. It's only a matter of time before they are rocked again.

More than 12 million Japanese choose to live in the Tokyo danger zone. They live there for the same reason that 16 million Californians make their homes next door to the world's largest fault line. In both places, the benefits of life there outweigh the fear of what will happen when the "Big One" comes.

Every day, the world's plates shift a little more. Every day, the pressure continues to build. Every day, Earth twitches—if not under Tokyo or Los Angeles, then somewhere else.

Chapter 5: Introduction

Imagine . . .

Sissano Lagoon,
northwest Papua New Guinea
Friday, July 17, 1998
6:30 P.M.

I**T CAME FROM NOWHERE.** The first thing Jacob heard was a low roaring in the distance. He was on the beach with the other kids. They were all studying the mysterious cracks that had opened up in the sand a little earlier.

It was the start of the long weekend and everyone was looking forward to the night's festivities. Jacob hoped a storm wasn't about to blow in and spoil the party.

The sea looked calm enough. There was a dark band on the horizon, but it might have been clouds. But they were miles away and there was scarcely any wind at all.

The roaring, however, grew steadily louder.

Jacob frowned. The dark band in the distance seemed to be getting bigger as well. By now, a large crowd had gathered on the beach. Jacob's parents were among the crowd. No one paid attention to the cracks now. All eyes were turned to the sea and the darkness rising above it like a thick black curtain.

Then Jacob finally realized what it was.

Water!

A huge wall of water was racing toward them.

He'd seen big waves before. But he'd never seen anything like this. Jacob glanced back at their house, among the palm trees at the edge of the lagoon. A wave that size would smash it to kindling.

He grabbed his mother's hand, pulling her away. "Run!" he shouted, barely able to make himself heard above the roar. "Run!"

His mother hesitated a moment, then turned and ran. She was clinging to Jacob with one hand and clutching his little sister, Anna, tightly to her chest with the other.

Everyone else was running, too. Some ran toward the shelter of the trees. Others ran blindly. Everyone was desperate to get away from the mountain of water churning and raging behind them.

Jacob glanced back to see the wave poised above them. It was like a huge, foam-crested hand, taller than the highest palm tree. Then it crashed down on them with a thunderous roar and snatched them into its fist.

Jacob tried to keep hold of his mother's hand, but it was wrenched away. He struggled against the dark, rolling water—unable to see, unable to breathe, tumbling over and over and over.

Something slammed into his chest. Jacob closed his arms around its hard, ridged surface. He held on with all his strength as the water slowly went back. Gasping, he gulped air into his aching lungs. Then he looked around.

He was high atop a coconut tree. Below him, the

beach where his village had been was strewn with broken trees and what was left of shattered houses. Steel bridges had been wrenched from their concrete piers. Jacob saw a few people struggling in the retreating water. Many more bobbed lifelessly or were scattered like driftwood along the sand.

He closed his eyes, pressing his face against the trunk of the palm. He was afraid to look too hard at the bodies. He didn't want to see his mother and father among them. Or Anna. Or any one of a hundred other friends and relatives.

He barely noticed when a second wave struck the tree, then a third. By then, he was beyond caring.

His village. His home. His family. His people. All were gone. The same sea that his father had fished for so many years had risen up and destroyed them.

There would be no party tonight.

Jacob wondered if there would ever be one again. . . .

Chapter 5
Wild Water

Everything in the story actually happened. It didn't just happen to a boy named Jacob. In fact, only a handful children survived the three deadly 30-foot waves that struck the coast of Papua New Guinea, on July 17, 1998.

Fifteen hundred bodies, young and old, were found among the wreckage. Thousands more vanished without a trace, most likely washed out to sea. In all, perhaps half of the 10,000 people who once lived on the shores of Sissano Lagoon lost their lives in the disaster.

Reporters who visited the scene said it looked like a giant comb had been raked across the land.

An Ocean on the Move?

Giant waves like the ones that totalled Sissano Lagoon in 1998 are known as tsunamis—sometimes called "tidal waves." Most are started by earthquakes. They can also be caused by undersea landslides or by volcanic eruption. The eruption at Krakatoa produced waves between 100 and 130 feet high.

When an earthquake hits the ocean floor, it makes ripples much like a stone does when you throw it into a pool of water. But the tsunamis caused by an earthquake are hundreds of miles long and several miles wide. They are huge walls of water that move at speeds of over 180 mph.

Waves of Destruction

Out at sea, where the water is deep, the waves are usually quite small. They may be only four inches high. But, as they get near land, the water gets shallower. The waves suddenly slow down. The water further out is still moving faster, so water piles up into a huge wave.

tsunami: (su-nah-me) A huge wave caused by an earthquake or other large disturbance; tidal wave.

This happens extremely fast. A tsunami can rise to heights of 100 feet in less than three seconds. And when it hits land, the breaking waves are immensely powerful. They leave behind widespread flooding and destruction. In low-lying areas, everything within a mile of the shore can be completely washed away.

Why Are Tsunamis So Dangerous?

One of the most frightening things about tsunamis is that they strike without warning. The quakes that cause tsunami often occur far out to sea. The tsunami may not even be seen by people on the shore. When shock waves from the July 17 quake reached seismographs in Japan, villages at Sissano Lagoon were already destroyed.

Tsunamis are almost impossible to detect in deep water. Ships can sail right across a passing tsunami without noticing anything at all.

The waves move so quickly that escape is often impossible. The first hint of approaching disaster is a high roaring sound in the distance, like that of a jet taking off. When you hear that sound, you have about 10 minutes to get at least a mile away from the shore and 115 feet above sea level. In lowland areas like Sissano Lagoon, there is no place to run.

Where Do Tsunamis Strike?

Tsunamis only form under certain conditions. The water has to be deep enough to form large, fast-moving waves. There has to be an earthquake, eruption, or undersea landslide to trigger one. Over 90 percent of all tsunamis recorded have occurred in the largest, deepest ocean in the world—the Pacific.

The Hawaiian Islands have been ravaged by more than 100 tsunamis since 1819. Tsunamis have swept the coasts of Alaska and California. Japan has also been badly hit. In 1896, one of the most destructive tsunamis ever recorded struck the port of Sanriku. It smashed more than 6,000 houses and killed close to 27,000 people.

Surging Storms

Tsunami-like waves can also occur during major storms. As a hurricane or cyclone passes over the ocean, the low pressure in its eye causes the water to bulge upward. This is known as a storm surge. When powerful winds drive these huge masses of water toward shore, they, too, cause widespread flooding and destruction in low areas.

Although the waves caused by storms aren't usually as big as genuine tsunamis, storm surges can still reach heights of 25 to 35 feet. A storm surge at least this big was responsible for most of the 500,000 deaths recorded in the great Bangladesh cyclone of 1970.

The Greatest Disaster of Them All?

Heavy rain is less spectacular than a tsunami or a storm surge. But flooding caused by rain and swollen rivers can be just as deadly. The single worst natural disaster in history may well be the great flood that occurred in northern China in September and October of 1887.

No one knows exactly how many people died. But it is believed that somewhere between 900,000 and 6 million lives were lost. When the great Yellow River overflowed its banks, some 40,000 square miles of countryside were under water. More than 300 villages were destroyed by the raging waters, which rose 65 feet above normal in places. At least another 2 million people were left homeless.

The aftermath of a tsunami

Large-scale flooding is a constant threat throughout the world. Each year, vast areas of land are drowned for weeks at a time beneath huge sheets of water.

In the country, floods cause extensive damage. Crops are ruined. Good farming soil is washed away, and huge numbers of livestock either drown or starve from lack of feed. In towns and cities, many homes are badly damaged and millions of dollars worth of property is destroyed.

Too Much of a Good Thing?

Every large river is surrounded by a flood plain. This plain can be more than 50 miles wide in places. A flood plain is actually part of the riverbed itself. Whenever an unusually large amount of water drains into the river, the flood plain fills up. Because the soil is richer there than anywhere, flood plains have been popular places for people to live and farm.

Aerial view of a flood

One great flood plain surrounds the Mississippi and Missouri rivers. Together, these rivers drain 155,000 billion gallons of water from the Midwest every year. The Mississippi flood plain covers an area of about 50 million acres. This includes some of the country's best farmland as well as the cities of New Orleans and St. Louis.

Whenever the rivers rise too high, these areas are at risk of being submerged. This has happened at least 50 times in the past 300 years. Many experts believe that flooding along the Mississippi poses a greater threat to people and property in the U.S. than the San Andreas fault.

Taming Old Man River

People have tried to control flooding on the Mississippi River for more than two centuries. Early settlers built dirt walls, known as levees, along its banks to try to hold back flood waters. Over the years, these walls were raised and strengthened until they extended for hundreds of miles on both sides of the river. The Mississippi, however, continued to flood.

In April 1927, winter rains sent torrents of water surging down the river. The Mississippi broke through the levees in 120 different places.

levee: A man-made bank beside a river used to prevent flooding.

Cars can get into trouble crossing flooded roads.

Millions of acres of land flooded to depths of 55 feet, and 750,000 homes were swamped. New Orleans was saved only by blasting a gap in the levee outside of the city to divert the water around it.

A year after another disastrous flood in 1937, the U.S. government began building. What they made became the world's most extensive flood-control system.

The system had two main features. Three hundred dams on rivers that feed the Mississippi would control the amount of water flowing into it. New levees up to 55 feet high would stretch along some 3,000 miles of riverbanks. Much of the work was done by U.S. Army engineers, but cities and towns also built levees.

A Losing Battle?

Despite everything that has been done to control flooding in the Mississippi Basin, the river still overflows its banks roughly once every ten years. The most recent flood was in 1993. After weeks of steady rain throughout June into July, rivers upstream of the Mississippi swelled to four or five times their normal size. In some places, over ten inches of rain was recorded in a single day.

All this water had to go somewhere. By mid-July, a 455-mile stretch of the Mississippi had overflowed its banks. At the same time, 635 miles of the Missouri river also flooded. Eight million acres of farmland were under water. Over half of the 1,400 levees that were built to hold back raging waters had been either damaged or destroyed.

Although most of the concrete levees around the major cities held, many cities barely escaped serious flooding.

In Hannibal, Missouri, town officials had calculated that the highest the river could possibly rise was 30 feet. They built a 31-foot levee just to be safe. As the waters started rising in July, they quickly added another three feet of sandbags to the top. The river eventually peaked at 32 feet. Another two feet and the city would have been

Flood gauge

completely under water.

By the time the floodwaters finally subsided, 50 people were dead and 70,000 were homeless. The total bill for the damage was estimated at more than $12 billion.

More Harm Than Good?

Trying to control floods may actually make things worse. In 1993, levees along the Mississippi actually caused the river water to rise higher and travel faster than it would have. This meant that in places where the levees gave way, the damage was enormous. The record water levels along the river would never have happened if the river had been allowed to spread into its flood plain.

Efforts to tame the mighty Yellow River in China have had much the same results. In 1998, a number of dams along the river had to be destroyed. Floodwaters were rising so steeply behind the dams that several cities were in danger of being completely swamped. When the dams were destroyed, mountains of water were suddenly sent rushing downstream. The water caused great damage to smaller towns and villages and drowned millions of acres of the country's richest farmland.

Why Take the Risk?

After the 1993 floods, one U.S. official suggested that certain towns on the Mississippi should be moved to higher ground. Levees could then be dismantled. The river could then use its natural flood plain in years of high rainfall. There would still be floods from time to time. But the water would spread much more slowly and peak at much lower levels. Most people living along the river, however, prefer to stay where they are and just hope that the levees hold.

More of the Same?

Floods are a natural part of a river's life cycle. They only become disasters when humans are in their path. This will happen more and more as the number of people living on flood plains grows.

Unlike earthquakes or volcanoes, floods are natural disasters people help to create. The more lands we clear for houses and farms, the less forest there is to soak up rainwater.

A recent survey found that the volume of water in the Mississippi has risen by 250 percent over the past 50 years.

Rivers everywhere are also showing increasing

volumes of water. Unable to cope with the extra run-off, they will overflow their banks more often. The results will be increasingly devastating.

Clearing forests makes flooding worse.

You'll probably never be swamped by monster waves the way Jacob was at Sissano Lagoon in the story. But a river near you could easily run over one day. If so, you may discover that water is one of nature's deadliest "weapons."

Imagine . . .

somewhere,
some day,
some time . . .

THE COUNTDOWN continues.
3:00:13 – 3:00:12 – 3:00:11 –
3:00:10 – 3:00:09...

You've been glued to the television
for days, just like billions of other
people around the world. At first,
CNN had to make do with computer
animations. Now they're showing live
feeds from the Hubble Space
Telescope. Last night, you could see
the asteroid clearly in the night sky.
It looked so small and
insignificant. Just a tiny dot of

light in an ocean of stars.

A week ago, only a handful of astronomers even knew the asteroid existed. It was merely a number in a catalog—2002 XF37. Merely one more chunk of rock floating harmlessly through space. In a few hours, it will slam into Earth. It will explode with the same force as a billion tons of TNT.

And your world will die.

It's like something out of an old sci-fi movie. Only there's no Bruce Willis to save the day. All you can do is sit in front of the television and count down the minutes to impact. There's nowhere to run, nowhere to hide. Your parents sit beside you on the couch, holding hands.

Their faces are pinched. Like you, they look on helplessly as the numbers on the screen grow ever smaller.

3:00:08–3:00:07–3:00:06–3:00:05–3:00:04 . . .

You don't dare go outside. There have been riots, and the army is keeping order. Looters have been shot. On the news, you've seen huge religious rallies. Weird doomsday cults have sprung up. There have been mass suicides.

For one group the asteroid is an alien spacecraft coming to take them to a better world. It isn't, of course. It's just 50 billion tons of rock whose path will soon cross with the tiny blue dot that is Earth.

No one knows exactly where it will hit. You and your family might survive impact. Even so, the collision will kick up huge clouds of dust. According to TV documentaries, the sun won't shine for months, maybe years. Crops and animals will die. There will be famine. Law and order will break down. Your safe, comfortable world will disappear.

You nestle closer to your parents. Your mother looks as if she's about to cry. You want to say everything will be all right. But that would be a lie. So you don't say anything. Instead, you stare at the television. You watch the drab gray rock tumble silently through space. The clock ticks down second by second.

3:00:03–3:00:02–3:00:01–3:00:00 . . .

You wait. . . .

Chapter 6
From Outer Space

THIS STORY MIGHT SOUND like science fiction. At the moment, that's exactly what it is. Experts, are almost certain that a giant asteroid has plowed into Earth at least once before, wiping out nearly all life. They also believe that it could happen again.

Movies like *Deep Impact* and *Armageddon* actually understate the effects of a large unearthly object hitting Earth. If something "the size of Texas" really were on a collision course with our planet, there would be no way of saving nearly all living creatures from extinction.

A crater from a meteor strike in Arizona

Fortunately, these events happen rarely—maybe once every 100 million years or so. The threat of such a disaster may make an exciting action movie, but it's not worth losing sleep over.

A Crippling Blow

What does worry many experts is something much smaller hitting us in the near future. Even an object only a few miles across could cause a lot of damage.

The number of people who might be killed by the impact would depend on where it occurred. Since most of Earth's surface is water, there's a good chance the impact would be in an ocean. It could trigger tsunamis 20 times larger than the one that swamped Sissano Lagoon. Within hours, most of Earth's low-lying areas would be completely drowned, including Los Angeles, New York City, and Tokyo.

Back to the Dark Ages?

The long-term effects of an impact would be devastating. Clumps of debris hurled into space by the explosion could fall back to Earth. As they passed through the atmosphere, these clumps would become red-hot. Many would burn up completely. Millions of others might rain down on forests and villages and cities across the globe.

Soon the entire world would be alight. Smoke and dust would blacken the sky. Without sunlight, no plants would grow for months, perhaps even years. Once food supplies started to run out, there would be mass starvation. Billions of people would die.

The world as we know it today would simply cease to exist. People who did survive would find themselves living the way people did 500 years ago, during the Dark Ages.

Where Do These Killer Rocks Come From?

If something does hit Earth one day, it will be either an asteroid or a comet. Asteroids are lumps of rock and metals that scientists think are left over from the formation of the universe billions of years ago.

Most asteroids are concentrated in a belt between Mars and Jupiter. They will never come anywhere near Earth. But a few hundred of them are circling the Sun in orbits that approach or cross Earth's own orbit. Called near-Earth objects (or NEOs), these asteroids are the possibly dangerous ones.

Scientists know of about 2,000 asteroids large enough to cripple our civilization. Only a very few are in orbits that might come close to Earth one day. Of the 245 asteroids whose paths have been charted, none are targeted toward Earth. That still leaves 1,755 potential killer rocks out there.

An Even Greater Danger?

Comets are chunks of loosely packed ice and dust about the size of a city. Comets travel in long orbits that can take them far outside the solar system. Unlike the asteroids, it is hard to know how many comets there are

Halley's comet

or whether they are headed our way.

Compared to the number of NEOs, there are far fewer comets on a path that would bring them close to Earth. However, comets travel much faster than asteroids. Their high speed means that a comet headed for Earth might not be discovered until two years before it strikes.

A comet would hit a lot harder than an asteroid, for the same reason that a high-speed snowball hurts more than one someone just tossed gently your way. When that snowball is ice and dust traveling at around 124,000 mph, it doesn't have to be big to cause a lot of damage.

What Are the Odds?

On May 21, 1998, a world expert on NEOs told the U.S. government he thought there was a

1-in-10,000 chance of a mile-wide asteroid or comet hitting Earth in the next 100 years.

But, there doesn't seem to be any pattern to asteroid and comet impacts. One is just as likely to hit in 2002 as 2222, or any other given year. The risk is present, but it is certainly not large.

Searching the Skies

There is one major difference between impacts and other natural disasters. We might actually be able to protect ourselves from a comet or asteroid. There are safety measures we can take.

First, we need to find out whether a mile-wide asteroid is headed our way. Scientists have called on NASA to fund a $60-million "*Spaceguard Survey*" aimed at finding 90 percent of potentially dangerous NEOs within the next ten years.

Although Spaceguard Survey would target larger asteroids, thousands of smaller ones would also be discovered at the same time. Small asteroids might not threaten civilization, but they would still cause

Spaceguard Survey:
A project designed to locate all potentially dangerous near-Earth objects and calculate their exact orbits.

widespread destruction if they hit populated areas.

The asteroid Gaspra

An asteroid no bigger than a house would explode with the same force as 15 million tons of TNT. One about that size struck the Tunguska river valley in Russia in 1908. It flattened forests ten miles in every direction. Imagine what it would have done to a major city like Washington, D.C.!

Could We Divert Disaster?

If we discovered that an NEO was headed our way, there are other measures we could take. The impact zone could be evacuated and food could be stored to help people survive the environmental disaster that would follow.

It's likely, however, that we'd be warned of any potential NEO impact many years in advance. This would give us time to do something about it.

We might explode a rocketload of powerful bombs in just the right place. That might alter the NEO's course so that it missed Earth by millions of miles. Only a small nudge would be needed, if it was done before the object got too close.

What Are We Doing About It?

Although the Spaceguard Survey is not up and running yet, the problem of NEOs is not being ignored. Several international conferences have addressed the issue. Scientists from all over the world have determined how to spot the most dangerous NEOs.

The easiest way to detect NEOs is by observing their reflected sunlight. This can be done with ground-based telescopes. More sophisticated methods are not necessary. We can reduce the threat of a comet or asteroid collision to 25 percent, just by looking.

But What If . . . ?

The chances of a catastrophic collision are so slim, most scientists say that it's not worth worrying about. But film studios and science-fiction writers like us to consider the question.

So just suppose . . . you found out that civilization was about to be destroyed. Civilizations have been destroyed before, by wars and natural disasters. However, none of them knew in advance that the end was coming.

How would people behave if they suddenly

learned that the world they knew would soon end? Would there be total panic? Would law and order completely break down? Would people steal whatever they could to have some chance of surviving? Or would they simply accept their fate and try to make the most of what little time they had left?

I'm not sure I know what I'd do. What about you? How do you think you'd react once the countdown started?

How would you spend your final few hours?

An artist's impression of an asteroid striking the surface of Earth

Where to from Here?

You've just read about natural disasters and how they affected people in their paths. Here are some ideas for finding out more about people dealing with disasters.

The Library

Some books you might enjoy include:
- *Hurricanes & Tornadoes*, by Neil Morris
- *Earthquakes*, by Neil Morris
- *Volcano*, by Patricia Lauber
- *Storms*, by Seymour Simon

TV, Film, and Video

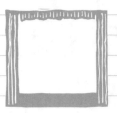

Watch TV listings for Public Broadcasting Station (PBS) programs about natural disasters, including National Geographic specials.
Ask at a video store or your library for films on natural disasters.

The Internet

Try key words such as *volcanos*, *natural disasters*, *hurricanes*, *tornadoes*, and *earthquakes*. The U.S. National Weather Service site, *www.nws.noaa.gov*, is a great source of information about storm disasters.

People and Places

Ask your family and friends if they've had experiences with natural disasters. Try to visit a meteorologist, or weather expert, at a local television station.

The Ultimate Fiction Book

Be sure to check out *Edge of Disaster*, the companion volume to *Earth Alert*. *Edge of Disaster* tells the thrilling story of a boy and his friends caught in a sudden volcano eruption.

Decide for yourself
where fact stops
and fiction begins.

Index